MW01701937

JEHOVAH'S DECREE

Says...

If you seek **God** early
in the morning surely *HE*
will wake *for you*, and though
your beginning was
small, *your* ending will
be *great*

ANA MALDONADO

Our Mission

Called to bring the supernatural power of God to this generation

Jehovah's Decree

ISBN: 978-1-59272-357-7

Edition April 2010

Project Director:	Addilena Torres
Cover Design:	Sergio Alvarado and Jessie Morales
Translation and Editorial Development:	Adriana Cardona and Henrry Becerra
Interior Design:	Jose Miguel Anhuaman

Published by:
ERJ Publicaciones
13651 SW 143 Ct., Suite 101, Miami, FL 33186
Tel: (305) 382-3171 - Fax: (305) 675-5770

Category: Prayer

PRINTED IN THE UNITED STATES OF AMERICA

Dedication

I dedicate this book to my precious heavenly Father for giving me the strength of His Holy Spirit to win battles in favor of His beloved Church. I thank Him for the perseverance He has given me to get up every morning to seek His presence. Everything I know, everything I am, and everything I do for my husband Guillermo Maldonado, for my children, Bryan and Ronald, and for my own life, I owe to those precious mornings with my Lord. I also dedicate it to the intercessors who continually pray for this ministry and for me—thank you for repairing the gap for us daily.

Acknowledgment

I consider prayer to be the most beautiful love language available to us. Grateful people purposefully thank God for all things, including those who serve and work in the ministry. The worst type of person one can encounter is an ungrateful person. Gratefulness is the most beautiful virtue a heart can possess. Gratefulness is a biblical virtue. A personal anecdote: One morning, my son, Ronald, woke up and told me, "Mommy, I am very grateful to my dad; that is why I love him because he sacrifices himself for the people." That is a grateful heart. Today, I thank all those who have the heart of a child; they will be abundantly blessed.

Index

Index

Prologue

I always rejoice when I am asked to write a prologue to recommend the writings of my spiritual sons and daughters, but this is a greater joy because it concerns someone I love more: my wife. My delight in doing so also comes from seeing my wife grow and mature in her calling. I know that everything written in this book is the real experience of a consecrated, dedicated, sacrificed, and audacious woman. Every day, early in the morning, she intercedes for the Church, for her family, and for the nations. I consider her to be a woman with a spiritual burden. She loves intercession and has divine revelation in this area, as well as in deliverance.

Three important points stand out in Jesus' prayers: He prayed in agreement with the Word, He prayed for His people, and His prayers were always answered. Likewise, Ana is one of those people whom the Lord has as His extension in the ministry of intercession. She prays according to the Word and for everything you will see in this book: the nations, the government, marriages, families, Israel, children, souls, finances, and more. I personally testify that, in all areas, God listens to and answers her prayers. I know few people in the Body of Christ with the grace and anointing to intercede, as my wife. One virtue I greatly thank her for and that I always appreciate and value is her commitment to pray for our children and for me, everyday. We are her number one priority. In fact, raising a protective barrier around the husband and children should be every woman's number one priority

Having said that, I feel more confident and willing to recommend this book; one birthed out of the spiritual deposits of a woman consecrated to God and very dear to my heart; a woman whom I love deeply. I am proud that this book will reach so many; it is a blessing. Furthermore, I declare that as the Lord answers my wife's prayers, He will also answer the prayers of those who read this book as they are activated in intercession. I sincerely recommend it. I am certain that as you read it, you will be touched and transformed.

Once again, I do not tire of expressing the happiness and joy it produces in me to write the prologue to a book that will bless so many people throughout the world. I wish for every reader to use these prayers and apply them to their lives as they activate themselves to bless all the people that God has put around them. Thank You, Lord, for the opportunity of writing this prologue for the most important person in the world to me, my wife!

Apostle Guillermo Maldonado
King Jesus International Ministry
Miami, FL. USA

Introduction

When the disciples asked Jesus to teach them to pray, He responded with the Lord's Prayer, which was to serve only as a guide to follow when praying to the Father. Jesus never meant for this prayer to be repeated verbatim; rather, through it, He made emphasis on the important points we need to present before the Lord, trusting the Father would hear our petitions.

The book you hold in your hands was created with the same intent: to serve as a guide when presenting yourself before the Father in prayer for your children, marriage, husband, and the calling you and your loved ones have within the Church; for your personal and financial needs, holiness, victory when doing spiritual warfare, and for any other need you might have. Perhaps, at first, you will have to read the prayers, but as you familiarize yourselves with the content, you will learn to pray in the same powerful way Jesus taught us. My intention in writing these prayers is not for you to practice vain repetition, but rather, for you to take the essence of the prayer and, based on the Word, declare and proclaim your needs before God.

The words you read in this book are actual prayers that have been declared early in the morning, in the company of God's people. These have been powerful journeys of prayer, intercession, deliverance, and spiritual warfare before God. The prayers you will read are loaded with the people's commitment, their tears, desires, and covenants with our heavenly Father and our beloved Jesus of Nazareth.

My work within the Body of Christ has always been to intercede for my husband, our children, the ministry God entrusted to us, and for the men, women, and children in our congregation. My strong calling to intercession has also served to help birth the calling of each person marked and separated by the Holy Spirit to share, together with my husband, the ministerial challenges we face.

Today, I invite you to join me in raising an altar of prayer to the Lord. Regardless of where you are, what you do for a living, your position in church, your social status, your level of education, or even if you are a new believer, God has a purpose and a glorious plan for your life. Remember, you are not what people say you are or even what you see in the mirror. You are what God's Word declares that you are.

Come and pray with me as a child of God, created in His image and likeness, washed by the blood of Christ, dead to sin the moment you welcomed Jesus to be your Lord and Savior, and raised with Christ when He conquered death and sin.

The Bible teaches that when two or more people are in agreement on any one thing, whatever they ask, believing, will be given to them. Today, I declare that you and I are in agreement, praying for the same things. Right now, begin to declare with me, knowing that our Father who is in Heaven is the living God; the one who sees, feels, hears, and acts on our behalf. He will give us everything we need according to His riches in glory in Christ Jesus; the results will amaze you!

One last request: I would like to hear from you and learn how God's supernatural power works in your life through prayer. I invite you to call our ministry and share your testimony.

God bless you!

Chapter 1

GOD'S WORD AS A WEAPON

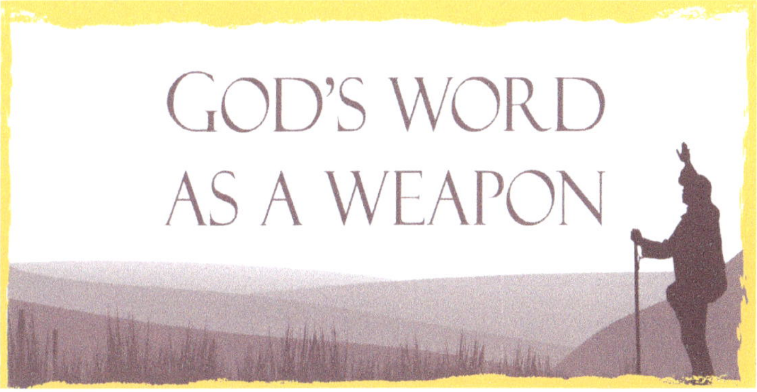

God's Word as a Weapon

It is crucial to understand the importance of praying according to the Word of God. Only the Bible protects us from making incorrect and emotional prayers; prayers that sound good to earthly ears but which are meaningless to God. Having said this, I invite the intercessors of the world to change the bad concept many have towards intercession. Though it is true that some pray incorrectly, it is also true that most intercessors are people full of the power of God to declare, decree, and establish His will on Earth. We pray correctly when we do so according to the Scripture, without trying to please the world and avoiding expressions that manipulate and control. The Word of God is the weapon that best protects us; it is the double-edged sword in our mouth that has the power to create and destroy, to bind and to loosen. The Word of God is a weapon that never fails and or returns void. On this day, I invite you to begin praying according to the Word of God. As written in the book of Acts, "We will give ourselves continually to prayer and to the ministry of the Word."

God's Word is the weapon that gives us the legal right to do everything Jesus did and more. God's word is sharper than any double-edged sword which penetrates until dividing soul and spirit and discerns the thoughts and intentions of the heart. It is the weapon that confirms He will give us what we ask for as long as we ask and go in His name.

"12 Most assuredly, I say to you, he who believes in Me, the works that I do he will do also; and greater works than these he will do, because I go to My Father. 13 And whatever you ask in My name, that I will do, that the Father may be glorified in the Son. 14 If you ask anything in My name, I will do."

John 14:12-14

....

....

....

....

God's Word is the weapon that gives us the power to destroy the enemy; it protects us against all adversity.

"19Behold, I give you the authority to trample on serpents and scorpions, and over all the power of the enemy, and nothing shall by any means hurt you."
Luke 10:19

God's Word is the weapon that empowers us to bind the evil works of the enemy and to loosen the blessings that are being held back.

"18Assuredly, I say to you, whatever you bind on earth will be bound in heaven, and whatever you loose on earth will be loosed in heaven."
Matthew 18:18

God's Word is the weapon that guarantees we shall receive everything God promised if we remain firm and steady.

"7If you abide in Me, and My words abide in you, you will ask what you desire, and it shall be done for you."
John 15:7

....

....

....

....

God's Word is the weapon that encourages and gives us the confidence and assurance that everything that seemed impossible for us is definitely possible for God.

"[27]But Jesus looked at them and said, 'With men it is impossible, but not with God; for with God all things are possible.'"
Mark 10:27

God's Word is the weapon that guarantees we can achieve absolutely everything if we believe God.

"[19]And my God will meet all your needs according to his glorious riches in Christ Jesus."
Philippians 4:19 (NIV)

God's Word is the weapon that makes it possible for us to claim the wealth and spoils that rightfully belong to us, according to the wealth possessed by our heavenly Father.

"[23]Jesus said to him, 'If you can believe, all things are possible to him who believes.'"
Mark 9:23

God's Word is the weapon that empowers us to obtain the wisdom of heaven and capacitates us to face every trial and adversity.

"[5]If any of you lacks wisdom, he should ask God, who gives generously to all without finding fault, and it will be given to him."
James 1:5 (NIV)

God's Word is the weapon that allows us to trust in His power to carry out His will, regardless of the enemy's plans against us.

"[20]Daniel answered and said: 'Blessed be the name of God forever and ever, for wisdom and might are His. [21]And He changes the times and the seasons; He removes kings and raises up kings; He gives wisdom to the wise and knowledge to those who have understanding. [22]He reveals deep and secret things; He knows what is in the darkness, and light dwells with Him.'"
Daniel 2:20-22

....

....

....

....

God's Word is the weapon that prospers all the things we do because God is always with us.

"[7]Only be strong and very courageous, that you may observe to do according to all the law which Moses My servant commanded you; do not turn from it to the right hand or to the left, that you may prosper wherever you go."
Joshua 1:7

Chapter 2

PERSONAL PRAYERS

Personal Prayers

The time we dedicate to our personal prayers will mark our level of consecration to the Lord. For that reason, it is important for us to surrender every area of our lives to God. Many are still living with problems of anger, egos, desires, and lasciviousness. Others are still in bondage to desires they have been unable to break; these often have to do with lust or the uncontrolled desire for material things which leads to the use of eroticism, sensuality, and dishonesty as weapons to reaching their objective. Because of this, I felt it was important to include in this personal devotional every area that makes us stumble in our walk with God. David said in Psalm 35, *"Judge me, O Lord my God, according to Your righteousness, and let them not rejoice over me; deliver me from deceitful and unjust men. Plead my cause with those who strive with me; fight against those who fight against me. Let those be put to shame and brought to dishonor who seek after my life; let those be turned back and brought to confusion who plot my hurt."* Today, I invite you to check your life, area by area, and consecrate it to the Lord. I am convinced that God will give you the victory.

I trust in God and abide under the shadow of the Almighty. Lord, You are my hope and strength. You deliver me from my enemies. You cover me with your feathers and protect me under Your wings. You are my shield and buckler. I shall not fear the terror by night, the arrows by day, or the pestilence that lurks in darkness. I will not fear death that destroys by day. Lord, I declare that a thousand may fall by my side and ten thousand at my right hand, but nothing shall touch me or hurt me.

"1He who dwells in the secret place of the Most High shall abide under the shadow of the Almighty. 2I will say of the LORD, 'He is my refuge and my fortress; My God, in Him I will trust.' 3Surely He shall deliver you from the snare of the fowler and from the perilous pestilence. 4He shall cover you with His feathers, and under His wings you shall take refuge. His truth shall be your shield and buckler. 5You shall not be afraid of the terror by night, nor of the arrow that flies by day, 6Nor of the pestilence that walks in darkness, nor of the destruction that lays waste at noonday. 7A thousand may fall at your side, and ten thousand at your right hand; but it shall not come near you."

Psalms 91: 1-7

Lord, in Your name, I bind the spirit of death, theft, kidnap, and destruction that the enemy might send against my life. Jesus, today, I receive the abundant life You have for me.

"[10]The thief does not come except to steal, and to kill, and to destroy. I have come that they may have life, and that they may have it more abundantly."
John 10:10

My beloved heavenly Father, in Your name, I declare that every prayer of manipulation, control, and witchcraft is pulverized right now. Lord, teach us to declare Kingdom prayers. Give us the wisdom to know when to open our mouths to speak so each word we utter is directed by Your Holy Spirit. Lord, I declare that every prayer I make is based and rooted in the fear of the Lord.

"[26]Likewise the Spirit also helps in our weaknesses. For we do not know what we should pray for as we ought, but the Spirit Himself makes intercession for us with groanings which cannot be uttered."
Romans 8:26

"[3]You ask and do not receive because you ask amiss..."
James 4:3

....

....

....

....

I bind all manmade plans and every attack created by the devil or sent from Hell against me or the Church of Christ. I declare that You, Lord, have the last word upon my life and over Your children.

"[33]The lot is cast into the lap, but its every decision is from the LORD."
Proverbs 16:33

Holy Spirit, help me to go before God's throne so I can worship my King, together with the 24 elders that remain prostrate in the heavens, giving Him tribute, honor, and glory. Lord, I join their worship declaring that You are holy, holy, holy. You are worthy. Today, Heaven and Earth become one to worship You in spirit and in truth.

"[10]The twenty-four elders fall down before Him who sits on the throne and worship Him who lives forever and ever, and cast their crowns before the throne, saying: [11]'You are worthy, O Lord, to receive glory and honor and power for You created all things...'"
Revelations 4:10, 11

"[24]God is Spirit, and those who worship Him must worship in spirit and truth."
John 4:24

....

....

....

....

Lord, teach us the mystery of Your will in our prayers and worship, and teach us to do Your will in our family, marriage, and ministry. Today, Lord, we take hold of Your will and allow it to be fulfilled in every step we take.

"[9]And he made known to us the mystery of his will according to his good pleasure, which he purposed in Christ".
Ephesians 1:9 (NIV)

Lord, I declare the true revelation of Heaven reaches Your people. I bind all false revelation; everything that comes from flesh and blood. Lord, raise me up in intercession with revelation, for Your honor and glory.

"[17]Jesus answered and said to him, 'Blessed are you, Simon Bar-Jonah, for flesh and blood has not revealed this to you, but My Father who is in heaven.'"
Matthew 16:17

I rebuke and cast out the painful memories of my past, and I receive the new and powerful things that You, Lord, have destined for my life. Right now, I activate Your grace to discern them and to move accordingly.

"[18]Forget the former things; do not dwell on the past. [19]See, I am doing a new thing! Now it springs up; do you not perceive it? I am making a way in the desert and streams in the wasteland."
Isaiah 43:18, 19

Lord, we connect all Kingdom prayers and declare that every prayer is spoken according to Your Word, Your heart, and Your thoughts. Right now, these are coming together before the throne of grace. Father, thank You because You send Your immediate answer from Heaven.

"[19]Again I say to you that if two of you agree on earth concerning anything that they ask, it will be done for them by My Father in heaven."
Matthew 18:19

Father, help us to be good administrators of the gifts and mysteries You deposited in us. Holy Spirit of God, give me the grace to be found faithful in everything the Father has entrusted to me.

"[1]Let a man so consider us, as servants of Christ and stewards of the mysteries of God. [2]Moreover it is required in stewards that one be found faithful." 1 Corinthians 4:1, 2

"[42]And the Lord said, "Who then is that faithful and wise steward, whom his master will make ruler over his household, to give them their portion of food in due season?"
Luke 12:42

Lord, pave my way, expand my territory, and make every step I take firm and secure. Keep me from falling, and make my path safe. Don't allow me to fall, and give me the victory in the midst of any circumstance that life sends my way.

"[36]You enlarged my path under me,
so my feet did not slip."
Psalms 18:36

Lord, fill me with Your Agape love, which is unconditional and able to uproot all lies, perversion, and deceit from the human heart. Fill my heart with Your love; the only one capable of casting out all fear, until I can be perfected in You.

"[9]The heart is deceitful above all things, and desperately wicked; who can know it?"
Jeremiah 17:9

"[18]There is no fear in love; but perfect love casts out fear, because fear involves torment. But he who fears has not been made perfect in love."
1 John 4:18

Lord, I need Your presence. I am nothing without Your Agape love. I plead Your mercy because of my weaknesses, and create in me a new heart. Don't leave me nor forsake me, and never take Your Spirit from me.

"[10]Create in me a clean heart, O God, and renew a steadfast spirit within me. [11]Do not cast me away from Your presence, and do not take Your Holy Spirit from me."
Psalms 51:10, 11

Lord, pass a burning coal through my mouth so that I might only speak Your words. Stop me from uttering falsehoods and keep vigil, with holy zeal, every word that I speak. Lord, in Your name, I declare that the words I speak restore the fallen, heal the sick, and bless all that hear me.

"[6]Then one of the seraphim flew to me, having in his hand a live coal which he had taken with the tongs from the altar. [7]And he touched my mouth with it, and said: 'Behold, this has touched your lips; Your iniquity is taken away, and your sin purged.'"
Isaiah 6:6, 7

Lord, help me to build up Your work with noble materials; with gold, silver, and precious stones so when the test by fire comes it will not be consumed, but rather, my work be found and proven to be valuable.

"[13]His work will be shown for what it is, because the Day will bring it to light. It will be revealed with fire, and the fire will test the quality of each man's work."
1 Corinthians 3:13 (NIV)

I put on the Armor of the Lord and am strengthened in its great power. I declare that no trick of the enemy can touch me and that on the dark days I will be able to resist, with firmness, until the end. Right now, I bring forth into the light of the Holy Spirit all lies of the devil and his evil attacks, and I declare these are dismantled, destroyed, demolished, and invalid by the power in the name of Jesus, His Word, and His precious blood.

"[10]Finally, be strong in the Lord and in his mighty power. [11]Put on the full armor of God so that you can take your stand against the devil's schemes."
Ephesians 6:10, 11 (NIV)

Lord, You are my shield, my refuge, my strength, and my help at all times. You descended and defended me when You heard my plea and rescued me from the hand of my enemies. For this and much more, I rejoice and praise You forever.

"[7]The LORD is my strength and my shield; my heart trusted in Him, and I am helped..."
Psalms 28:7

Lord, I speak to the dry bones of my spiritual calling and declare that every plan You created for my life, which I have allowed to die, lives again, right now! I breathe upon these dry bones—my spiritual calling—the breath of God's life and declare these are revived once more. Lord, I prophesy according to Your Word: "Holy Spirit, come from the four winds and breathe upon these dead bones, and they shall live!"

"[4]Then he said to me, 'Prophesy to these bones and say to them, 'Dry bones, hear the word of the LORD! [5]This is what the Sovereign LORD says to these bones: I will make breath enter you, and you will come to life.'"
Ezekiel 37:4, 5 (NIV)

Lord, train me for war and prepare me for battle. Spirit of God, teach me to walk the extra mile and give me the strength and vigor to go with You further than it is required of me.

"[1]Blessed be the LORD my Rock, who trains my hands for war, and my fingers for battle."
Psalms 144:1

"[41]And whoever compels you to go one mile, go with him two."
Matthew 5:41

Lord, today I align myself to Your words. I receive Your authority to uproot, destroy, ruin, and dismantle every plan of the wicked one and every assignment of the enemy against my life and Your people.

"9Then the LORD put forth His hand and touched my mouth, and the LORD said to me: 'Behold, I have put My words in your mouth. 10See, I have this day set you over the nations and over the kingdoms, to root out and to pull down, to destroy and to throw down, to build and to plant.'"
Jeremiah 1:9, 10

I activate the splendor of God's glory upon my life and declare that wherever I go, the people will heed the call to repentance and salvation which I will speak in His name. The majesty of God's glory in me brings the lost to the feet of Christ.

"3The Gentiles shall come to your light, and kings to the brightness of your rising. 4Lift up your eyes all around, and see: They all gather together, they come to you; your sons shall come from afar, and your daughters shall be nursed at your side."
Isaiah 60:3, 4

In Your name, Lord, I declare that greater is He who lives in me—Christ Jesus—than any circumstance in my life. Furthermore, with You by my side, I am invincible because nothing and no one can come against me.

"[4]You, dear children, are from God and have overcome them, because the one who is in you is greater than the one who is in the world."
1 John 4:4 (NIV)

"[31]What then shall we say to these things? If God is for us, who can be against us?"
Romans 8:31

I declare that today the Lord will crush Satan and cause him to submit and be firmly held under my feet. Today, the Lord covers us with His grace and favor and empowers us to destroy every evil work wherever we go.

"[20]And the God of peace will crush Satan under your feet shortly. The grace of our Lord Jesus Christ be with you. Amen."
Romans 16:20

....

....

....

....

I am an impenetrable fortress. I am made of bronze, and the enemy cannot infiltrate or pierce my life. I declare that I am strong, and I have control and authority over every circumstance because my heavenly Father, Jesus of Nazareth, and the Holy Spirit placed me on Earth to exert lordship, to subdue, and to exercise dominion over my surroundings.

"[18]For behold, I have made you this day a fortified city and an iron pillar, and bronze walls against the whole land—against the kings of Judah, against its princes, against its priests, and against the people of the land."
Jeremiah 1:18

The blood of Jesus speaks for me and saves my life. His blood delivers my mind, my conscience, my subconscious and cleanses every thought, imagination, my body, soul, and spirit.

"[22]But you have come... [24]to Jesus the Mediator of the new covenant, and to the blood of sprinkling that speaks better things than that of Abel."
Hebrews 12:22, 24

I nail my old nature —my carnal mind and my earthly nature— to the Cross of Calvary. I declare, with the power and the authority Jesus gave me, that Jesus is enthroned in everything I do.

"[20]I have been crucified with Christ; it is no longer I who live, but Christ lives in me; and the life which I now live in the flesh I live by faith in the Son of God, who loved me and gave Himself for me."
Galatians 2:20

"[7]Because the carnal mind is enmity against God; for it is not subject to the law of God, nor indeed can be."
Romans 8:7

I declare that I will never accept or join the mentality or ways of this world, but rather, my understanding will be renewed each day until I am able to prove and live in God's perfect will.

"[2]And do not be conformed to this world, but be transformed by the renewing of your mind, that you may prove what is that good and acceptable and perfect will of God."
Romans 12:2

....

....

....

....

I declare that every diabolic demand raised against me has to go; it must disappear. Likewise, oppression, premature aging, and back-bending stress have to go, right now! I declare that every unholy prayer of witchcraft sent against me is now cancelled and removed; it is rebuked and cast out, and the only burden I carry is the one Jesus gives me which is light and easy.

"[29]Take My yoke upon you and learn from Me, for I am gentle and lowly in heart, and you will find rest for your souls. [30]For My yoke is easy and My burden is light."
Matthew 11:29, 30

I declare that every generational curse against my life and every wicked word spoken against me are cancelled, right now! In the powerful name of Jesus Christ, I declare that no curse or evil word will ever take a foothold in my life. I declare it inoperative, right now!

"[13]Christ has redeemed us from the curse of the law, having become a curse for us (for it is written, 'Cursed is everyone who hangs on a tree')."
Galatians 3:13

In the powerful name of Jesus Christ, I bind the spirits of torment and worry and declare that my faith is rooted in the Lord. I know He will do much more for us, His children, than what He does for the birds of the air.

"[25]Therefore I tell you, do not worry about your life, what you will eat or drink; or about your body, what you will wear. Is not life more important than food, and the body more important than clothes? [26]Look at the birds of the air; they do not sow or reap or store away in barns, and yet your heavenly Father feeds them. Are you not much more valuable than they?"
Matthew 6:25, 26 (NIV)

Get behind me, Satan! I know that greater is He who is in me, Jesus of Nazareth, than he who is in the world. Therefore, I declare the mundane thoughts sent by Satan will not cause me to stumble because my eyes are firmly set on God and things above.

"[23]...Get behind Me, Satan! You are an offense to Me, for you are not mindful of the things of God, but the things of men."
Matthew 16:23

Lord, I declare that You loosen Your power and strength against my enemies. Almighty God, thank You for redeeming us through the blood of the Lamb without sin.

"[10]Now these are Your servants and Your people, whom You have redeemed by Your great power, and by Your strong hand."
Nehemiah 1:10

Dear God, I ask that You fill me with Your love, wisdom, and power to accomplish all that You have placed before me: my marriage, my children, the ministry, and the nations.

"[10]Give me wisdom and knowledge, that I may lead this people, for who is able to govern this great people of Yours?"
2 Chronicles 1:10 (NIV)

I bind every spirit of accusation that has ever come against my life, and I declare myself free, in the name of Jesus, because the Lord has erased my rebellion and no longer remembers my sin.

"[25]I, even I, am He who blots out your transgressions for My own sake; and I will not remember your sins."
Isaiah 43:25

Chapter 3

PRAYERS FOR CHILDREN AND FAMILIES

Prayers for Children and Families

I often hear parents and their children complain about each other; the reasons are countless, and yet, with all their talking, the one thing they lack is communication. Parents rarely speak to each other and children avoid talking to their parents; sadly, worse than not talking to each other is their lack of relationship and communication with God. Today, I call parents to pray for their children. Providing food and clothing is not enough. Children need our prayers. Even if we feel they are not the best children or they have gone astray, we should not judge or reject them. Instead, we must open our hearts to know their concerns, problems, dreams, and desires. It is paramount that parents cry out for their children and protect them through prayer. They are being attacked on all sides: in schools, by their friends, and even through television. The messages they receive incite them to misbehave; it is time to change that. Before we try to take up the titanic task of changing the world, let us, first, help our children and prevent them from getting swallowed up by the current of this world. Let us raise an altar of prayer for our children!

I cover my children with the blood of the Lamb and declare that on this day, they are protected by the covenant established by the blood of Jesus. Furthermore, I declare they are protected in their comings and goings; the justice of God goes before them, and the glory of the Lord is their rear guard. I forbid the enemy from oppressing them with fear, worry, or anguish. Every man or woman who approaches them must have the fear of the Lord. I declare my children are under the Lord's care. He will satisfy their soul during times of drought and strengthen their bones. I declare my children are like a watered garden, whose waters do not fail.

"[11]The LORD will guide you continually, and satisfy your soul in drought, and strengthen your bones; you shall be like a watered garden, and like a spring of water, whose waters do not fail."
Isaiah 58:11

Lord, I uproot from my children anything not planted by You; every bad influence picked up in school and all words of advice given under false wisdom. I uproot bad friendships, acquaintances, and any tree around them that bears no fruit for Your Kingdom.

"13But He answered and said, 'Every plant which My heavenly Father has not planted will be uprooted...'"
Matthew 15:13

In the powerful name of Jesus of Nazareth, I declare and establish the protection and safety of my family and finances. I speak peace, joy, and tranquility over my children. Lord, according to Your Word, I ask for Your grace to help us surrender to You and resist the devil; only then will the devil have no option but to flee.

"7Therefore submit to God. Resist the devil and he will flee from you."
James 4:7

"27Nor give place to the devil."
Ephesians 4:27

....

....

....

....

I declare my children and every member of my family are held in safety in the palm of Your hand. I further declare that no weapon formed against my children or young people will prosper. I trust in You, and because of that trust, I know I will never be shamed.

"[17]No weapon formed against you shall, and every tongue which rises against you in judgment You shall condemn..."
Isaiah 54:17

I declare my children will fulfill the purpose and calling You placed in their lives, according to Your divine plan. Your inheritance belongs to them because they were adopted through Jesus Christ, according to the plan established by the Father.

"[10]For we are His workmanship, created in Christ Jesus for good works, which God prepared beforehand that we should walk in them."
Ephesians 2:10

I declare that my children, those who were lost or separated from Your light and are living in darkness, return home today!

"[32]...we should make merry and be glad, for your brother was dead and is alive again, and was lost and is found."
Luke 15:32

I declare my children dwell in the secret place of the Most High, where they are safe and secure. I raise a powerful, impenetrable shield around them where no harm can come to them. With authority, I declare they will not fear the terror that lurks in darkness and nothing and no one can harm them. No one who believes in You will be shamed!

"[1]He who dwells in the secret place of the Most High shall abide under the shadow of the Almighty."
Psalms 91:1

"[4]He shall cover you with His feathers, and under His wings you shall take refuge; His truth shall be your shield and buckler. [5]You shall not be afraid of the terror by night, nor of the arrow that flies by day, [6]Nor of the pestilence that walks in darkness... [7]A thousand may fall at your side, and ten thousand at your right hand; but it shall not come near you."
Psalms 91:4-7

I declare my children hate what God hates and love what God loves. They walk victoriously in the name of truth, humility, and justice.

"[20]If someone says, 'I love God,' and hates his brother, he is a liar; for he who does not love his brother whom he has seen, how can he love God whom he has not seen."
1 John 4:20

"[7]You love righteousness and hate wickedness; therefore God, Your God, has anointed You with the oil of gladness more than Your companions."
Psalms 45:7

I declare my children are blessed in their comings and goings. I declare that if the enemy rises against them, he will come one way but will have to flee before You seven ways.

"[6]Blessed shall you be when you come in, and blessed shall you be when you go out. [7]The LORD will cause your enemies who rise against you to be defeated before your face; they shall come out against you one way and flee before you seven ways."
Deuteronomy 28:6, 7

I declare my children will not fear evil because You will protect them every day of their lives. You will give them courage and place them in high standing if anyone or anything tries to intimidate them.

"[4]Yea, though I walk through the valley of the shadow of death, I will fear no evil; for You are with me; Your rod and Your staff, they comfort me. [5]You prepare a table before me in the presence of my enemies..."
Psalms 23:4, 5

Lord, I declare that nothing and no one can separate my children, my family, or myself from Your presence and immense love.

"[38]For I am persuaded that neither death nor life, nor angels nor principalities nor powers, nor things present nor things to come, [39]nor height nor depth, nor any other created thing, shall be able to separate us from the love of God which is in Christ Jesus our Lord."
Romans 8:38, 39

I declare the Lord has sent His angel to protect and keep us safe. This angel encamps around my children, my marriage, my home, and my finances because it all belongs to Him—those who seek the Lord will never lack what they need.

"[7]The angel of the LORD encamps all around those who fear Him, and delivers them."
Psalms 34:7

"[21]Then the LORD sent an angel who cut down every mighty man of valor, leader, and captain in the camp of the king of Assyria..."
2 Chronicles 32:21

Lord, in Your name, I bind Satan's lies and all mundane spirits. I declare my family and I will worship and serve You, and You alone.

"[8]Again, the devil took Him up on an exceedingly high mountain, and showed Him all the kingdoms of the world and their glory. [9]And he said to Him, 'All these things I will give You if You will fall down and worship me.' [10]Then Jesus said to him, 'Away with you, Satan! For it is written, 'You shall worship the LORD your God, and Him only you shall serve.'''"
Matthew 4:8-10

Lord, I declare our youth will not lose their way because Your commandments are enthroned in their hearts.

"[9]How can a young man cleanse his way? By taking heed according to Your word. [10]With my whole heart I have sought You; oh, let me not wander from Your commandments! [11]Your word I have hidden in my heart, that I might not sin against You."
Psalms 119:9-11

I declare the Lord will guard our children's comings and goings, today and forever.

"[8]The LORD shall preserve your going out and your coming in from this time forth, and even forevermore."
Psalms 121:8

Lord, I declare young people will not be conformed to this world; they will trust in You and mount up with wings like eagles.

"[31]But those who wait on the LORD shall renew their strength; they shall mount up with wings like eagles, they shall run and not be weary, they shall walk and not faint."
Isaiah 40:31

I declare this generation will find safety and provision in You, not in drugs, alcohol, or friends.

"[1]I will lift up my eyes to the hills—from whence comes my help? [2]My help comes from the LORD, who made heaven and earth."
Psalms 121:1, 2

Lord, pour out Your grace upon each family on Earth, and may Your grace overflow where sin, to this day, had the upper hand.

"[20]Moreover the law entered that the offense might abound. But where sin abounded, grace abounded much more."
Romans 5:20

Lord, I declare our youth will testify and confirm to future generations: "For as long as I have lived, I have never seen the righteous abandoned or in need because the Lord has always provided."

"[25]I have been young, and now am old; yet I have not seen the righteous forsaken, nor his descendants begging bread."
Psalms 37:25

Lord, I declare deliverance for every young person in spiritual bondage, for every one that today lives in darkness and places of captivity, seduced, harassed, tormented, weakened, and enslaved by demons. In the precious name of Jesus of Nazareth, I loosen these young people from their bondage. I deliver them and send them forth to carry out God's purpose for their lives!

"[44]...he who had died came out bound hand and foot with graveclothes, and his face was wrapped with a cloth. Jesus said to them, 'Loose him, and let him go.'"
John 11:44

Lord, in Your name, I bind, rebuke, and cast out the spirit of rejection and independence from our children. I declare unity and restoration in their lives as the Lord makes the hearts of parents return to their children and the hearts of children return to their parents.

"[6]And he will turn the hearts of the fathers to the children, and the hearts of the children to their fathers..."
Malachi 4:6

....

....

....

....

Lord, I loosen the spirit of prophecy over my children. In the name of Jesus, I declare their eyes will be opened to see heavenly visions. Lord, pour out Your Spirit upon them!

"[28]And it shall come to pass afterward that I will pour out My Spirit on all flesh; Your sons and your daughters shall prophesy, Your old men shall dream dreams, Your young men shall see visions."
Joel 2:28

"[11]'I raised up some of your sons as prophets, and some of your young men as Nazirites. Is it not so, O you children of Israel?' Says the LORD."
Amos 2:11

In Your name, Lord, I light a lamp at my children's feet. No shadow of sin, sickness, or death will ever touch them. I declare each step they take will always be guided by the light of Your Word.

"[105]Your word is a lamp to my feet and a light for my path."
Psalms 119:105 (NIV)

....

....

....

....

Right now, Lord, I raise up the shield of faith and put out every fiery arrow sent by the enemy; every attack in the form of a family crisis, divorce, fighting, deceit, and/or abuse against my children.

"[16]Above all, taking the shield of faith with which you will be able to quench all the fiery darts of the wicked one."
Ephesians 6:16

Chapter 4

PRAYERS FOR THE PRIESTHOOD

Prayers for the Priesthood

Someone once wrote that when women pray the heavens are opened, and when men pray hell trembles. This is a great truth. Nevertheless, raising priests in our house, in church, and in society is a special calling for women. Whether you are a pastor, a businesswoman, a mother, a wife, or a daughter, this is a biblical mandate. In Genesis, God assigned woman the mission of being her husband's ideal helper. As such, women are called to have an intimate relationship with God in order to present prayers and pleas for the priesthood in her home, only then will we see a true reform, for if the man carries out his corresponding role as a priest, the family and nation will be transformed by the power of God. In the Old Testament, priests had to minister to God and present Him with sacrifices, offerings, and prayers for the tribes (families) of Israel. For that reason, every priest carried on his chest twelve precious stones signifying that after God, his priority was his family. Sisters, unite with me! Let us raise in prayer the priesthood of our husbands and children!

Lord, in Your name, I declare the same spirit of warfare and boldness that was upon David is upon our priesthood. I raise them up as men of valor; committed and trained for war in body, soul, and spirit. Furthermore, when the enemy rises against us, they will rise and declare, "Who are you to touch my family, my finances, my home, or my inheritance?" I declare these men will crush and destroy any giant that dares to challenge them, and they will do it in the name of Jesus!

"26 David asked the men standing near him, 'What will be done for the man who kills this Philistine and removes this disgrace from Israel? Who is this uncircumcised Philistine that he should defy the armies of the living God?' 45 David said to the Philistine, 'You come against me with sword and spear and javelin, but I come against you in the name of the LORD Almighty, the God of the armies of Israel, whom you have defied."
1 Samuel 17:26, 45 (NIV)

I declare righteous, honest, honorable, pure, and noble thoughts in the priesthood of this house.

"[8]Finally, brethren, whatever things are true, whatever things are noble, whatever things are just, whatever things are pure, whatever things are lovely, whatever things are of good report, if there is any virtue and if there is anything praiseworthy—meditate on these things."
Philippians 4:8

Lord, I declare that today, everything that was misaligned in the priesthood of this house is aligned according to Your divine will and to the decrees of Your Word.

"[5]Every valley shall be filled and every mountain and hill brought low; the crooked places shall be made straight and the rough ways smooth."
Luke 3:5

I declare that all men have the mind of Christ and live their lives focused on their calling. I declare that confusion will never enter their minds or hearts.

"[16]For who has known the mind of the Lord that he may instruct him? But we have the mind of Christ."
1 Corinthians 2:16 (NIV)

I declare our priests are seating in their rightful place, and that Jesus positioned them in heavenly places in order to show us His kindness.

"[6]And raised us up together, and made us sit together in the heavenly places in Christ Jesus."
Ephesians 2:6

Devil, I accuse you before the heavenly Father for confusing the priesthood through the spirit of Leviathan. I accuse you for provoking and tempting man's ego; for causing restlessness and attacking and assaulting our priests. Because of what you have done, I rebuke you devil. I crush your head and declare your defeat.

"[1]In that day the LORD with His severe sword, great and strong, will punish Leviathan the fleeing serpent, Leviathan that twisted serpent; and He will slay the reptile that is in the sea."
Isaiah 27:1

"[14]You broke the heads of Leviathan in pieces, and gave him as food to the people inhabiting the wilderness."
Psalms 74:14

I declare the men in our House have holy zeal for God's laws; that their priesthood produces a powerful and righteous generation empowered with a legacy of blessings for Your children.

"[2]His descendants will be mighty on earth; the generation of the upright will be blessed. [3]Wealth and riches will be in his house, and his righteousness endures forever."
Psalms 112:2, 3

I declare there is no room for double-mindedness in the Body of Christ. I declare this illegal! I loosen spiritual stability and reliability in the Church.

"[7]For let not that man suppose that he will receive anything from the Lord; [8]he is a double-minded man, unstable in all his ways."
James 1:7, 8

Lord, I loosen supernatural hunger and thirst for your presence over the priesthood; a yearning that only You can satisfy. I further declare they will rise and stand before You, the Living God.

"[1]As the deer pants for the water brooks, so pants my soul for You, O God. [2]My soul thirsts for God, for the living God. When shall I come and appear before God?"
Psalms 42:1, 2

Lord, I know that in the vastness of the desert, You raise up a cloud by day and a pillar of fire by night. You light the way and protect the men in my home and in the Church. Lord, I know You will never leave them nor forsake them. Guide them through the path you have predestined for them.

"[21]And the LORD went before them by day in a pillar of cloud to lead the way, and by night in a pillar of fire to give them light, so as to go by day and night."
Exodus 13:21

Lord, I declare every man to be royal priesthood, chosen and dedicated for Your service and ministry. As such, they are not slaves of the world, of sin, or of any man; they serve justice and are consecrated for Your exclusive use. These men gather the harvest of holiness and eternal life.

"[18]And having been set free from sin, you became slaves of righteousness. [22]But now having been set free from sin, and having become slaves of God, you have your fruit to holiness, and the end, everlasting life."
Romans 6:18, 22

....

....

....

....

I place a veil of protection upon the eyes of the priesthood in the Church, with the blood of Jesus. I further declare that their eyes are Your eyes and that Your light shines through them. Lord, I loosen understanding upon their lives so they can recognize that their bodies are the temple of Your Holy Spirit.

"[34]The lamp of the body is the eye. Therefore, when your eye is good, your whole body also is full of light. But when your eye is bad, your body also is full of darkness."
Luke 11:34

"[16]Do you not know that you are the temple of God and that the Spirit of God dwells in you?"
1 Corinthians 3:16

Lord, I place a demand for holiness upon our priesthood. In the delegated authority I received from God, I activate the call for holiness that Jesus placed upon their lives, declaring they are holy in every area of life, as Jesus is holy.

"[16]Because it is written, 'Be holy, for I am holy.'"
1 Peter 1:16

I declare that the priesthood in the Church of Christ experiences the same level of desire and need that Isaiah felt and experienced, to be in God's presence. I further declare that while the Holy Spirit reigns in their lives, they shall seek You before sunrise and find You.

"[9]With my soul I have desired You in the night, Yes, by my spirit within me I will seek You early ..."
Isaiah 26:9

Lord, plant trees of righteousness in every Christian home; priests willing and able to establish and carry out Your commands in their homes so Your name can be glorified.

"[3]...That they may be called trees of righteousness, the planting of the LORD, that He may be glorified."
Isaiah 61:3

Lord, in Your name, I nail the old man (my flesh) to the Cross. Jesus, I declare that all fleshly desires and passions in our priesthood are crucified.

"[24]And those who are Christ's have crucified the flesh with its passions and desires."
Galatians 5:24

....

....

....

....

Lord, in Your name, I raise up a priesthood that will worship You in spirit and in truth; one that will exalt You from the depths of their hearts. Lord, I declare Your priesthood is free of religiosity, vain glory, or carrying out manmade mandates. Rather, they will live to carry out Your directives as they hold on to the desires of Your heart.

"[13]Therefore the Lord said: 'Inasmuch as these people draw near with their mouths and honor Me with their lips, but have removed their hearts far from Me, and their fear toward Me is taught by the commandment of men.'"
Isaiah 29:13

Lord, I raise up men after God's own heart, in our families, churches, and communities. I declare they are wise leaders and governors, a royal priesthood willing and able to guard Your commandments.

"[14]But now your kingdom shall not continue. The LORD has sought for Himself a man after His own heart, and the LORD has commanded him to be commander over His people, because you have not kept what the LORD commanded you."
1 Samuel 13:14

....

....

....

....

Lord, loosen wisdom and discernment upon Your priesthood as You did for Salomon, David's son. Help them to govern with righteousness and in line to Your commandments. Lord, I declare, in the name of Jesus, that they are the head and not the tail, able to establish divine order in all that You entrust them to carry out.

"[9]So give your servant a discerning heart to govern your people and to distinguish between right and wrong. For who is able to govern this great people of yours?"
1 Kings 3:9 (NIV)

Lord, from among your priesthood, raise up an army of men of valor, with the same resolve and endurance as Gideon and his men. I declare these men have the tenacity and courage to victoriously endure and cross over any adversity they might encounter.

"[4]When Gideon came to the Jordan, he and the three hundred men who were with him crossed over, exhausted but still in pursuit."
Judges 8:4

Lord, I declare the priesthood You raise up in this generation is like that of Aaron and his sons. Every man will be part of the royal priesthood, consecrated and anointed to serve You. Lord, You will anoint them, and they shall be called a holy nation.

"30 And you shall anoint Aaron and his sons, and consecrate them, that they may minister to Me as priests."
Exodus 30:30

Chapter 5

PRAYERS FOR WOMEN

Prayers for Women

I often come across women of all ages and conditions who, due to the struggles they faced when they were younger, grow up and face more problems in their marriages or other areas of their lives. This causes conflicts, traumas, and inner pains. The most frequent are emotional problems, including unforgiveness, frustration, and loneliness, as well as mental problems like confusion and anxiety. Added to these are family problems that lead to divorce. As such, it is extremely urgent for women to receive inner healing and deliverance, so they may rise and fulfill God's purpose for them. The apostle Paul was aware of this when he wrote to the Philippians, "For I know that this will turn out for my deliverance through your prayer and the supply of the Spirit of Jesus Christ." What he said is that when we pray, we give the Spirit of God freedom to intervene in people's lives, restoring everything they need. It is time for us to use the weapons God has given us, and begin to decree His Word under the guidance of the Holy Spirit. Woman, get up! God wants to deliver you today!

Lord, in Your name, I declare that virtuous, fearless women, unafraid of adverse circumstances, will rise up and stand firm and unmoved; women that resist adversity though they were abandoned to care for their children alone; women who in their loneliness know how to protect; who in the midst of inclemency still defend; women who laugh at the future because they know the best is yet to come. These women are bold, confident, and doubly clothed with the strength You give them.

"[21]She is not afraid of snow for her household, for all her household is clothed with scarlet. [25]Strength and honor are her clothing; she shall rejoice in time to come."
Proverbs 31:21, 25

Lord, in Your name, I declare You raise up women prophets, judges, and government leaders in our cities, states, and countries; bold, courageous, and influential women apt to lead Your people to great victories.

"[4]Now Deborah, a prophetess, the wife of Lapidoth, was judging Israel at that time. [5]...And the children of Israel came up to her for judgment. [9]So she said, 'I will surely go with you; nevertheless there will be no glory for you in the journey you are taking, for the LORD will sell Sisera into the hand of a woman.'"
Judges 4:4, 5, 9

Lord, in Your name, I declare the Church equips disciples, liken to Deborah, capable of shutting down every destructive plan created by the enemy against them, their families, nations, churches, and their callings. These women are strong, courageous, intelligent, and ready to defend the fruit of their womb.

"[21]But Jael, Heber's wife, picked up a tent peg and a hammer and went quietly to him while he lay fast asleep, exhausted. She drove the peg through his temple into the ground, and he died."
Judges 4:21 (NIV)

Lord, in Your name, I call forth women prophets and apostles equipped with power and authority to destroy every evil work and capable of crushing the devil's head.

"[15]And I will put enmity between you and the woman, and between your seed and her Seed; He shall bruise your head, and you shall bruise His heel."
Genesis 3:15

Lord, in Your name, I declare that, although the world might try to debilitate Your children, You will strengthen the women. Lord, Your people will never perish because You multiply and protect the fruit of their womb and prosper their families.

"[18]So the king of Egypt called for the midwives and said to them, 'Why have you done this thing, and saved the male children alive?' [19]And the midwives said to Pharaoh, 'Because the Hebrew women are not like the Egyptian women; for they are lively and give birth before the midwives come to them.' [20]Therefore God dealt well with the midwives, and the people multiplied and grew very mighty."
Exodus 1:18-20

Lord, in Your name, I declare that from among Your people, You call forth women that love You and whose desire is to serve You and You alone. I further declare they are blessed with divine health, and because of their service, they will not suffer the devastation of sterility in any area of their lives, and the fruit of their womb will forever be blessed!

"25So you shall serve the LORD your God, and He will bless your bread and your water. And I will take sickness away from the midst of you. 26No one shall suffer miscarriage or be barren in your land..."
Exodus 23:25, 26

Lord, in Your name, I curse the spirit of sterility that has attacked Your daughters and deposit in their womb seeds of blessings that will produce children who will lovingly serve You.

"3And the Angel of the LORD appeared to the woman and said to her, 'Indeed now, you are barren and have borne no children, but you shall conceive and bear a son.'"
Judges 13:3

....

....

....

....

Lord, in Your name, I declare that intelligent, beautiful, decisive, self-assured women, capable of fasting and praying to see Your will be done on Earth, rise and persevere. I declare these women have a defined calling and purpose, and their greatest desire is to please You, regardless of any risk or danger this might create in their lives.

"[15]Then Esther told them to reply to Mordecai: [16]'Go, gather all the Jews who are present in Shushan, and fast for me; neither eat nor drink for three days, night or day. My maids and I will fast likewise. And so I will go to the king, which is against the law; and if I perish, I perish!'"
Esther 4:15, 16

Chapter 6

PRAYERS FOR MARRIAGE

Prayers for Marriage

Today, it is easy to get married one day and divorced the next over something we dislike. A wave of divorces is taking place in our society; hence, the importance to seek the Lord's help on this matter. As an institution, the family finds itself in the emergency room and the prognosis is unfavorable, and only God can save it from this terrible plague that affects the couple, the children, and even the elders and widows. The shamelessness of men and women who choose to have an adulterous relationship, without regarding the consequences, should drive us to pray for our families. To those who are united in marriage, the Lord commands to remain united. If your family is well, then pray that nothing bad comes over it. If you are facing hardships in your marriage, then pray without ceasing. God is the only one that will give you the victory; the only one that delivers us from adversity. If this book is in your hands, it is because God is calling you to pray for marriages; to be someone who raises hedges of protection for your home and the homes of God's people; one who will stand in the gap, as in Ezekiel 22:30. Pray for your marriage! God wants to enter your house in a mighty way!

Lord, I declare Christian marriages are a threefold cord when Jesus is part of their relationship. The three are one as God the Father, the Son, and the Holy Spirit are one. My God, they are one in You: the husband, the wife, and You. Right now, I loosen the anointing, power, strength, and resistance of the threefold cord over every marriage among Your people.

"[12]Though one may be overpowered by another, two can withstand him. And a threefold cord is not quickly broken."
Ecclesiastes 4:12

Lord, I declare that marriage relationships have steel structures; these relationships will never be broken by crisis or disagreements. I declare that marriages are unbreakable and made to resist every test and trial sent by the world.

"[10]Now to the married I command, yet not I but the Lord: A wife is not to depart from her husband. [11]...and a husband is not to divorce his wife."
1 Corinthians 7:10, 11

Lord, I declare that no plan of the enemy can touch or destroy those who are married. In the name of Jesus of Nazareth, I destroy every spirit of division and contempt and establish unity, as written in God's Word.

"[8]And the two shall become one flesh; so then they are no longer two, but one flesh. [9]Therefore what God has joined together, let not man separate."
Mark 10:8, 9

....

....

....

....

I declare the unity of the Father, the Son, and the Holy Spirit is upon all who are married, and this makes them one in You.

"[4]There is one body and one Spirit..."
Ephesians 4:4

"[10]Have we not all one Father? Has not one God created us? Why do we deal treacherously with one another by profaning the covenant of the fathers?"
Malachi 2:10

Lord, I declare that no serpent's venom can contaminate the homes of God's children; it is eliminated and destroyed right now. I declare that against all venom created to separate there is a powerful antidote: the blood of our Lord Jesus Christ. I declare every serpent of division looking to crawl into marriage relationships is burned alive by the fire of the Lord.

"[5]But he shook off the creature into the fire and suffered no harm."
Acts 28:5

....

....

....

....

Lord, I declare we live according to Your Word and not in line with this world's vain glory. We live and walk by the Spirit, and the fruit of the Spirit fills our marital life.

"[22]But the fruit of the Spirit is love, joy, peace, longsuffering, kindness, goodness, faithfulness, [23]gentleness, self-control. Against such there is no law."
Galatians 5:22, 23

Lord, I declare every husband is the head of household and every wife the ideal helper —the shoulders that hold the head high. Lord, I declare it was Your plan to create us this way, and this is the Biblical order that must be observed by those who are married and claim to love You. The man is the head of his wife, as Jesus is the head of the Church.

"[22]Wives, submit to your husbands as to the Lord. [23]For the husband is the head of the wife as Christ is the head of the church, his body, of which he is the Savior."
Ephesians 5:22, 23 (NIV)

As a married couple, my spouse and I stand firm, in one voice, and declare, "Lord, we make ourselves available to You. We will go wherever You send us."

"[8]Also I heard the voice of the Lord, saying: 'Whom shall I send, and who will go for Us?' Then I said, 'Here am I! Send me.'"
Isaiah 6:8

Lord, I declare there is mutual respect between husbands and wives, and the love they share will last for eternity.

"[33]Nevertheless let each one of you in particular so love his own wife as himself, and let the wife see that she respects her husband."
Ephesians 5:33

Chapter 7

PRAYERS FOR THE CHURCH

Prayers for the Church

This is a call to the Church of Christ; a call to the male and female pastors who love the Lord and want to do His will. During the many trips I have made to the nations to preach His Word, I have noticed that when leaders rise up to care for their people in prayer and intercession, as Abraham and Moses did, the enemy will send many violent attacks against them. I say this because I have experienced it and continue to do so. For that reason, I exhort you as my brothers and sisters to not give up, despite the persecution, the problems, and the circumstances. Renew your strength and keep praying and interceding for your churches; do not dismay because this is the only way for the Lord to intervene, strengthen, and keep His Church ready for battle. God has given us power and authority to trample serpents and scorpions. Let us keep praying and interceding! Let us go together from a level of prayer and worship to one of spiritual warfare; one that destroys every work of evil and purifies the airs, so that the Spirit of God may show His supernatural power.

In the name of Jesus, I position fiery torches around our church and decree that no evil shall enter it; no demons or any type of evil meditation can rise against it. I further declare, in the name of Jesus, that every spirit of division, spiritual coldness, and deviation has to rot, cease, and desist its operations, right now! I declare these spirits will not enter the church, and every spy sent by the enemy is now taken captive and placed under submission to the obedience of Jesus Christ.

"[5]Casting down arguments and every high thing that exalts itself against the knowledge of God, bringing every thought into captivity to the obedience of Christ."
2 Corinthians 10:5

In the name of Jesus, I declare that walls of fire will stand firm and blazing around this church and the vision You have given it. I further declare that no one, absolutely no one, can come against this church!

"[5]'For I,' says the LORD, 'will be a wall of fire all around her, and I will be the glory in her midst.'"
Zachariah 2:5

"[18]And on this rock I will build my church, and the gates of Hades will not overcome it."
Matthew 16:18 (NIV)

In the name of Jesus, I declare Your servants will never look back once they decide to place their hands on the plow.

"[62]But Jesus said to him, 'No one, having put his hand to the plow, and looking back, is fit for the kingdom of God.'"
Luke 9:62 (NIV)

....

....

....

....

In the name of Jesus, right now, I crush every serpent that wants to rise against the Church. I squash, destroy, and cancel every infernal stronghold that has risen against Your Church, and I declare the victory is ours over the territory You gave us.

"[19]Behold, I give you the authority to trample on serpents and scorpions, and over all the power of the enemy, and nothing shall by any means hurt you."
Luke 10:19

In the name of Jesus, I declare Your people shall eat of the fruit of life and not of death. I further declare they will have abundant life, divine health and healing, and overflowing wealth, as they become your channels of life and blessings for others.

"[20]From the fruit of his mouth a man's stomach is filled; with the harvest from his lips he is satisfied. [21]The tongue has the power of life and death, and those who love it will eat its fruit."
Proverbs 18:20, 21 (NIV)

In the name of Jesus, I declare the ministry goes from glory to glory and from victory to victory, by grace and mercy of the Holy Spirit.

"[18]...being transformed into the same image from glory to glory, just as by the Spirit of the Lord."
2 Corinthians 3:18

In the name of Jesus, I declare Your fiery arrows force the enemy to step back. I raise up a hedge of fire around the intercessors and activate them for war. Every Pharaoh and his army must die in the depth of the sea because the Lord opens the Red Sea in favor of His Church, the churches under spiritual covering, and His people—I see the arrows of the Lord surrounding and defending the churches under spiritual covering.

"[5]'For I,' says the LORD, 'will be a wall of fire all around her, and I will be the glory in her midst.'"
Zachariah 2:5

"[15]He sent out arrows and scattered them; lightning bolts, and He vanquished them."
2 Samuel 22:15

....

....

....

....

In the name of Jesus, I declare the church is like a tree that will never die, dry up, or stop bringing forth fruit because the living water that nourishes it comes from Heaven.

"[8]He will be like a tree planted by the water that sends out its roots by the stream. It does not fear when heat comes; its leaves are always green. It has no worries in a year of drought and never fails to bear fruit."
Jeremiah 17:8 (NIV)

Chapter 8

PRAYERS FOR FINANCES

Prayers for Finances

Since the beginning of creation, God's purpose has been for man to lack nothing. In fact, He placed man in the Garden of Eden where His provision flowed ceaselessly and where man had a perfect relationship with Him. Nevertheless, man's sin and disobedience caused misery to reach our lives and ruin our finances. Today, it is sad to see people who busy themselves with listening to news from the stock market, surveys, and economic analysts, but who have yet to pay attention and hear the voice of God. The Bible is rich with examples of men and women who were prospered by God due to their tithes and offerings; this was the case with Abel, Abraham, Isaac, and Jacob. If in the Old Testament God considered the offerings valuable, then the same holds true in the New Testament. In the new pact, Jesus carried our poverty so that we could receive all the blessings of the pact with God. If you tithe and give offerings with joy, if you are a good steward of your house and business, and if you pray believing God, then He will surely rise up and bless you. Furthermore, He will return and multiply everything the enemy took from you. I believe in the promises of God. Dare to believe with me!

Listen well spirit of Mammon, you that bring debt to God's people. I cut off your tentacles which entrap people into unnecessary and emotional purchases. I bind you in the name of Jesus! Spirit of Mammon, you will not dictate what I will do with my money! I declare all my debts cancelled. I am debt-free, and I declare healthy finances over God's children. Money will not enslave me, but rather, it will serve to meet my needs.

"24No one can serve two masters; for either he will hate the one and love the other, or else he will be loyal to the one and despise the other. You cannot serve God and mammon."
Matthew 6:24

I declare that the finances of the people and my own are secure, regardless of what experts on the economy report. I further declare that my finances overflow in abundance because I am faithful in bringing my tithes and offerings to the altar. I decree that the windows of Heaven are always open, and there will always be abundance of wealth in my home, family, and country.

"[10] 'Bring all the tithes into the storehouse, that there may be food in My house, and try Me now in this,' says the LORD of hosts, 'If I will not open for you the windows of heaven and pour out for you such blessing that there will not be room enough to receive it.'"
Malachi 3:10

I declare prosperity over my life and family because of my obedience.

"[2] And all these blessings shall come upon you and overtake you, because you obey the voice of the LORD your God: [4] Blessed shall be the fruit of your body, the produce of your ground and the increase of your herds, the increase of your cattle and the offspring of your flocks."
Deuteronomy 28:2, 4

....

....

....

....

I declare that Jesus became poor so that I, through His poverty, might become rich.

"9For you know the grace of our Lord Jesus Christ, that though He was rich, yet for your sakes He became poor, that you through His poverty might become rich."
2 Corinthians 8:9

I declare abundant blessings, unlimited resources, and overflowing wealth because I honor the Lord with my finances. In the powerful name of our Lord Jesus Christ, I prophesy that the wealth of the unbelievers will pass to the hands of the righteous, right now!

"9Honor the LORD with your possessions, and with the firstfruits of all your increase; 10So your barns will be filled with plenty, and your vats will overflow with new wine."
Proverbs 3:9, 10

"22A good man leaves an inheritance to his children's children, but the wealth of the sinner is stored up for the righteous."
Proverbs 13:22

I declare that as Jesus multiplied the fish and the bread and fed five thousand men, not counting women and children, the multiplication of our finances will be evident in our homes and we shall never be in need.

"[41]And when He had taken the five loaves and the two fish, He looked up to heaven, blessed and broke the loaves, and gave them to His disciples to set before them; and the two fish He divided among them all. [42]So they all ate and were filled. [43]And they took up twelve baskets full of fragments and of the fish. [44]Now those who had eaten the loaves were about five thousand men."
Mark 6:41-44

I declare that neither the bin of flour nor the jar of oil will be used up. There will always be food in my pantry and no one in my family shall suffer hunger.

"[14]For thus says the LORD God of Israel: 'The bin of flour shall not be used up, nor shall the jar of oil run dry, until the day the LORD sends rain on the earth.'"
1 Kings 17:14

Holy Spirit, I recognize that without Your help, I will be unable to establish any new business or make good investments. I further declare that You fill me with wisdom, understanding, and discernment to know which business transaction to begin and which to end. I surrender to your leading and declare that every business venture I commit to will be entirely led by You.

"[2]The Spirit of the LORD shall rest upon Him, the Spirit of wisdom and understanding, the Spirit of counsel and might, the Spirit of knowledge and of the fear of the LORD."
Isaiah 11:2

I declare that the Lord rebukes the devourer of our finances. He fights for us! The nations will say we are blessed because we are called to be fertile, favored, and blessed ground into which all that is planted and invested will prosper.

"[11]'And I will rebuke the devourer for your sakes, so that he will not destroy the fruit of your ground, nor shall the vine fail to bear fruit for you in the field,' [12]And all nations will call you blessed, for you will be a delightful land,' Says the LORD of hosts."
Malachi 3:11, 12

Lord, I align myself to your thoughts and ways. In the name of Jesus, I declare that all Your plans to prosper my family and I, and to give us hope, will be carried out to completion.

"[9]For as the heavens are higher than the earth, so are My ways higher than your ways, and My thoughts than your thoughts."
Isaiah 55:9

"[11]'For I know the plans I have for you,' declares the LORD, 'plans to prosper you and not to harm you, plans to give you hope and a future.'"
Jeremiah 29:11 (NIV)

Lord, in Your name, I stretch my hand over any sea of adversity, circumstances, and crisis that might try to attack my life. Lord, I declare that new paths open up that will lead me to the promises and inheritance You have prepared for me.

"[16]But lift up your rod, and stretch out your hand over the sea and divide it. And the children of Israel shall go on dry ground through the midst of the sea."
Exodus 14:16

....

....

....

....

Chapter 9

PRAYERS FOR THE GOVERNMENT

Prayers for the Government

The condition of our society is a clear sign of how much we need to pray in favor of our rulers. Hypocrisy, corruption, mismanagement, unfaithfulness, lack of values, falsehood, failure to keep promises, power abuse, manipulation, and more are only a few of the words that describe what takes place, daily, in the world of politics in this and other countries. The personal crises experienced by the rulers of all nations affect millions of people around the world. Nevertheless, today, God places a demand on us to take up our corresponding responsibility. It is time for us to stand in prayer for other countries and ask that the will of God come to pass over each one. It is time for us to ask for better leadership for our nations. It is time to touch God's heart and ask Him to raise men and women committed to His Word and principles; people ready to pray for the destiny of His people. Through our prayers, God can influence the hearts of these men and women to make the right decisions and produce communities that will live in peace and become an inheritance for future generations.

I declare, in Your name, that every wicked spirit that moves in the sphere of the Supreme Court in this country is now paralyzed. I bind it, rebuke it, and cast it out. Father, in the name of Jesus, I go against the strong man that moves in the circles of influence in politics. I bind every demonic spirit of illegality and compromise that impairs governmental decisions. I bind all personal agendas that want to rise over and above the legitimate welfare of the people and this nation. I bind the spirit of partiality and other wicked spirits sent to oppress, delay or confuse the President of this great nation, Congress, governors, mayors, and any other person that works to serve Your people.

"[19]And I will give you the keys of the kingdom of heaven, and whatever you bind on earth will be bound in heaven, and whatever you loose on earth will be loosed in heaven."
Matthew 16:19

I declare the judgment of God is upon communism; this political doctrine will not penetrate or contaminate our country of ____________. Lord, I declare and decree that Your Kingdom and Government invades South and Central America, Africa, China, India, Europe, the Middle East, and every other nation around the globe. I declare that Your Kingdom completely destroys and eradicates the enemy, and Your whirlwind causes the evil ones to perish in their own wickedness.

"19See, the storm of the LORD will burst out in wrath, a whirlwind swirling down on the heads of the wicked."
Jeremiah 23:19 (NIV)

I declare the president of each nation around the world is presented before You today, by us and by their own people. I loosen the fear of God upon their lives and ask that You, Lord, stir within them the need to govern and live their lives according to divine wisdom and not human schemes and protocols.

"7The fear of the LORD is the beginning of knowledge..."
Proverbs 1:7

....

....

....

....

Lord, today I declare the peace that surpasses all understanding upon every politician, chosen by You to govern from a place of eminence, in service to Your people. I further decree that together, we will live quiet and tranquil lives, in peace and harmony.

"[1]Therefore I exhort first of all that supplications, prayers, intercessions, and giving of thanks be made for all men, [2]for kings and all who are in authority, that we may lead a quiet and peaceable life in all godliness and reverence. [3]For this is good and acceptable in the sight of God our Savior."
1 Timothy 2:1-3

I declare that all power and authority was given to us to bind every tongue that curses Miami, Florida, the United States of America, and my country _______. Furthermore, I bind every stronghold of darkness and the mouths of those who curse the president of this nation or the leaders in my country.

"[17]...and every tongue which rises against you in judgment You shall condemn..."
Isaiah 54:17

I declare that today, every heart of stone present in the government of all nations, The United Nations (UN), Organization of American States (OAS), and North Atlantic Treaty Organization (NATO) is transformed into a heart of flesh, according to Your Word.

"[26]I will give you a new heart and put a new spirit in you;
I will remove from you your heart of stone
and give you a heart of flesh."
Ezekiel 36:26 (NIV)

I declare that everything the President of the United States touches is blessed and prospered. He is the head and not the tail, first and not last, above and not below, and every land he sets his foot on will be won for Your Kingdom and glory.

"[13]And the LORD will make you the head and not the tail; you shall be above only, and not be beneath, if you heed the commandments of the LORD your God, which I command you today, and are careful to observe them."
Deuteronomy 28:13

"[3]Every place that the sole of your foot will tread upon I have given you, as I said to Moses."
Joshua 1:3

....

....

....

....

I declare the presidents of all nations are good-hearted people. Your Kingdom and the fulfillment of Your will shall be done upon their lives, and You give them grace and favor to do Your will on Earth.

"10 Your kingdom come. Your will be done on earth as it is in heaven."
Matthew 6:10

Chapter 10

PRAYERS TO WIN SOULS

Prayers to Win Souls

Jesus, the Son of God, became a man and paid a high price on the Cross for the salvation of the lost. Those who received Christ are obligated to pray for the Gospel to be preached in every nation. Your prayers can move God's mighty hand to reach the lost. Pray for His will to be done and for His mercy and the truth of His salvation to be known. You have a covenant with God that says, "Believe on the Lord Jesus Christ and you and your household will be saved" (Acts 16:31); this pact gives you the legal right to remind God about His promise. If you are separated from the Lord, repeat this prayer and make a new start: "Heavenly Father, I recognize that I am a sinner and that my sin separates me from you. I freely repent from all of my sins and confess Jesus as my Lord and Savior. I believe Jesus died for my sins and that God, the Father, raised Him from the dead. Jesus, I ask you to come into my heart and change my life. I renounce all covenants with the world, the enemy, and my flesh. If I die right now, when I open my eyes, I will be in your arms. Amen!"

I declare that the Church of Christ rises in every continent, in every country, and in every city: in the North, South, East, and West. Lord, You call Your children to go to the fields and gather the harvest which is ripe for harvest. In Your name, Lord, I place a demand for workers to rise and carry out this task, as You have commanded.

"[35]Do you not say, 'Four months more and then the harvest'? I tell you, open your eyes and look at the fields! They are ripe for harvest."
John 4:35 (NIV)

I declare the voice of the Church of Christ reaches every lost soul throughout the Earth, removing the veil that blinds their understanding. Furthermore, I declare that the voice of His Church penetrates and changes their mentality as it reveals that the one and only path to salvation is called Jesus Christ of Nazareth.

"[4]...whose minds the god of this age has blinded, who do not believe, lest the light of the gospel of the glory of Christ, who is the image of God, should shine on them."
2 Corinthians 4:4

I declare that all lost souls must fall to their knees in the presence of the one and only true God, and their tongues must confess that Jesus is the Lord and Savior of their lives.

"[10]That at the name of Jesus every knee should bow, of those in heaven, and of those on earth, and of those under the earth, [11]and that every tongue should confess that Jesus Christ is Lord, to the glory of God the Father."
Philippians 2:10, 11

....

....

....

....

I declare that God's Word will be preached in every corner of the globe as proof that Your second coming is at hand.

"[14]And this gospel of the kingdom will be preached in all the world as a witness to all the nations, and then the end will come."
Matthew 24:14

"[15]And He said to them, 'Go into all the world and preach the gospel to every creature.'"
Mark 16:15

"[9]...If anyone preaches any other gospel to you than what you have received, let him be accursed."
Galatians 1:9

I declare we have the boldness and audacity to advance the Kingdom of God and to win back the lost with force.

"[12]And from the days of John the Baptist until now the kingdom of heaven suffers violence, and the violent take it by force."
Matthew 11:12

....

....

....

....

I declare that You, Lord, seek and find the lost sheep. You gather them back into Your flock and rescue them from dark places where they were scattered.

"[11]For thus says the Lord GOD: 'Indeed I Myself will search for My sheep and seek them out. [12]As a shepherd seeks out his flock on the day he is among his scattered sheep, so will I seek out My sheep and deliver them from all the places where they were scattered on a cloudy and dark day."
Ezekiel 34:11, 12

I declare the people preach the Gospel of Jesus with their heads held high, and You, Lord, will give us the victory by saving the lost. Lord, don't allow anyone to shame us.

"[37]Yet in all these things we are more than conquerors through Him who loved us."
Romans 8:37

"[11]For the Scripture says, 'Whoever believes on Him will not be put to shame.'"
Romans 10:11

....

....

....

....

I declare that for each life the devil stole from this house, for each death he caused, hundreds of new souls will be added to the Kingdom of God. I proclaim these lives are taken back from the enemy's claws. Lord, deliver them from the devil's grasp!

"[21]I will save you from the hands of the wicked and redeem you from the grasp of the cruel!"
Jeremiah 15:21 (NIV)

"[21]I will also tear off your veils and deliver My people out of your hand, and they shall no longer be as prey in your hand. Then you shall know that I am the LORD."
Ezekiel 13:21

I declare the Angel of the Lord goes to and fro throughout the nations of the Earth, stirring the waters to save, heal, and deliver, not only one but every person who is still lost.

"[4]For an angel went down at a certain time into the pool and stirred up the water; then whoever stepped in first, after the stirring of the water, was made well of whatever disease he had."
John 5:4

....

....

....

....

I declare You have not given us a spirit of fear but of power, love, and a sound mind. Therefore, every time I open my mouth it will be to testify of what You have done in my life and to preach Your Word with boldness and power.

"[7]For God has not given us a spirit of fear, but of power and of love and of a sound mind."
2 Timothy 1:7

I declare that when we cast our nets, to the North, South, East, and West, these will overflow with people who have firmly decided to enter the Kingdom of God. Jesus ordained it!

"[6]And He said to them, 'Cast the net on the right side of the boat, and you will find some.' So they cast, and now they were not able to draw it in because of the multitude of fish."
John 21:6

Chapter 11

PRAYERS AGAINST THE SPIRIT OF JEZEBEL

Prayers Against the Spirit of Jezebel

The Church around the world has not fully realized the strong influence exerted by the spirit of Jezebel. The Bible teaches about Jezebel in the book of Kings and in Revelation, and through the prophet Elijah, it warns us of this strong demonic influence. Though the spirit of Jezebel has historically been linked to women, when it attacks, it does not discriminate genders. It is a spirit that incites, challenges, and seduces people to do what is wrong before God and the authorities He has appointed. Its main goal is to disrupt order, overthrow authority, and provoke evil. This spirit infiltrates to disobey the authority in the church, the family, and the nations. Jezebel is a spirit that uses seduction, fornication, and idolatry to manipulate and control. The Lord is challenging you today to continually renounce every form of "jezebelic" influence and stay watchful to guard your spiritual authorities through prophetic intercession. Let us unite and together, we will dethrone Jezebel!

I put on the Armor of the Lord: the helmet of salvation, the breastplate of righteousness, and the belt of truth. I take the shield of faith and the sword of the spirit, and I declare that my feet are fitted with the Gospel of peace. I submerge my children and my family in the blood of my Lord, Jesus Christ, and I declare that no pestilence or fiery dart of the enemy shall by any means touch them, the Church, or my brothers and sisters in the faith. I declare that no pestilence or plan formed against the daughter churches or those under spiritual covering will prosper. Jezebel, I forbid you to touch them! I paralyze your evil actions and decree that no plan against us will prosper!

"[11]Put on the whole armor of God, that you may be able to stand against the wiles of the devil."
Ephesians 6:11

I declare that every work of the devil, every hellish and satanic assignment, and the devil's prophets, dry up just like the fig tree that Jesus caused to dry up.

"[19]And seeing a fig tree by the road, He came to it and found nothing on it but leaves, and said to it, 'Let no fruit grow on you ever again.' Immediately the fig tree withered away."
Matthew 21:19

My spirit worships You, Lord. Today, I declare, with the power and authority You have given me, that we are the righteousness of God on Earth, and His righteousness terminates all injustice.

"[18]...for we do not present our supplications before You because of our righteous deeds, but because of Your great mercies."
Daniel 9:18

"[21]For He made Him who knew no sin to be sin for us, that we might become the righteousness of God in Him."
2 Corinthians 5:21

Jezebel, you filthy snake, I bind your words and shut your mouth! I curse you to slither on the ground, and there you shall remain. Your mouth will be filled with dust, and silent you shall remain for eternity.

"[14]...you are cursed more than all cattle, and more than every beast of the field. On your belly you shall go, and you shall eat dust all the days of your life."
Genesis 3:14

Lord, in Your name, I uproot every tree of wickedness planted by Satan. I declare that every demonic spirit is placed in bondage, confused, and silenced. Lord, I present before Your presence the intercessors and King Jesus International Ministry, and I decree that we take authority over the first heaven, the second heaven, and even under the Earth. We take authority over the air, and we bind the strongholds, the principalities, and the governors of darkness. In Your name, Lord, we destroy every wicked thing that resides in the heavenlies.

"[12]For we do not wrestle against flesh and blood, but against principalities, against powers, against the rulers of the darkness of this age, against spiritual hosts of wickedness in the heavenly places."
Ephesians 6:12

I bind and rebuke Jezebel and her diabolical plans. I decree confusion in the enemy's camp, over the spirit of control and manipulation, and the spirit of antichrist.

"[20]Then Saul and all his men assembled and went to the battle. They found the Philistines in total confusion, striking each other with their swords."
1 Samuel 14:20 (NIV)

Elijah declared before Baal's prophets that the one and only God would cause fire to descend from heaven. Likewise, I declare, with the delegated authority God has given me, that the fire of the Lord will descend and consume every altar that has or ever will be erected for idol-worshipping.

"[38]Then the fire of the LORD fell and consumed the burnt sacrifice, and the wood and the stones and the dust, and it licked up the water that was in the trench. [39]Now when all the people saw it, they fell on their faces; and they said, 'The LORD, He is God! The LORD, He is God!'"
1 Kings 18:38, 39

Jezebel, I decree you will eat the dust of the Earth. Dogs shall feast on you! I bind your witchcraft and every spirit of manipulation you have raised against God's people. All works of the occult are now destroyed! Jesus has you under His feet and continues to destroy you and your works. In Jesus' name, all mind control, seduction, and witchcraft are destroyed and God's people rejoice in the victory.

"[10]The dogs shall eat Jezebel on the plot of ground at Jezreel, and there shall be none to bury her.'"
2 Kings 9:10

"[37]And the corpse of Jezebel shall be as refuse on the surface of the field, in the plot at Jezreel, so that they shall not say, 'Here lies Jezebel.'"
2 Kings 9:37

Lord, by the power in Your name, in Your blood, and in Your Word, every mind and spirit that refuses to worship You is now cancelled and stirred into confusion; every rebellious spirit is now imprisoned and held captive.

"[24]...the LORD looked down from the pillar of fire and cloud at the Egyptian army and threw it into confusion."
Exodus 14:24 (NIV)

Chapter 12

PRAYERS FOR THE NATIONS

Prayers for the Nations

When God created the Earth, He did so with a specific purpose. Upon completion, He saw it was good, pleasing, and perfect. Nevertheless, Adam and Eve's rebellion, corruption, and their anxiety to live independently from God resulted in the generational harvest of curses that manifest through hatred, division, envy, enmity, sickness, pain, and death. Man has raised borders between cities and nations and violently closed the doors to God in schools and in many homes. For this reason, the Holy Spirit within us cries out daily, seeking available vessels; humans who want to be used by God to restore our nations so that He may birth the plans He established for your country and mine. Today, I invite you to join me, every day, in prayer and supplication for this nations and all other nations in the world. Together, we will see God's glory manifest everywhere, and those who see it will not be able to deny God's favor for us. They will surely say, "Surely this great nation is a wise and understanding people."

Lord, I humbly come before Your presence in repentance and ask Your forgiveness for every sin committed by the people in my nation. I ask You to forgive even those sins committed by my ancestors to the third and fourth generation. I declare that You, Lord, will descend and heal our land.

"[14]If My people who are called by My name will humble themselves, and pray and seek My face, and turn from their wicked ways, then I will hear from heaven, and will forgive their sin and heal their land."
2 Chronicles 7:14

Lord, I declare that Your glory will fill the Earth, and it will be seen by all the nations. Your glory will cover every state, country, and territory. These nations will be won for Christ and become an inheritance of the Kingdom of God for our children.

"[21]But truly, as I live, all the earth shall be filled with the glory of the LORD."
Numbers 14:21

Lord, I declare the enemy will never touch, block, or steal the prayers made by Your people. I further declare that the tears and clamor of Your people of every race, tongue, and nation purchased by the blood of Jesus are safely kept in a gold bowl, where they will remain sealed before Your throne of grace.

"[8]Now when He had taken the scroll, the four living creatures and the twenty-four elders fell down before the Lamb, each having a harp, and golden bowls full of incense, which are the prayers of the saints."
Revelations 5:8

I activate the angels of the Lord, with sharpened swords, to punish our enemies and send fiery darts to destroy every stronghold created by the devil. Lord, in your name, I activate your angels to judge the nations. By the finger of the Lord, I penetrate the devil's camp and paralyze it, bind it, and cast it out, in the name of Jesus of Nazareth.

"15 He shall call upon Me, and I will answer him; I will be with him in trouble; I will deliver him and honor him. 16 With long life I will satisfy him, and show him My salvation."
Psalms 91:15, 16

Lord, I declare the nations of the Earth are blessed. They are holy nations and a royal priesthood. They are Your own special people, and every man and woman in those nations proclaim the wonders performed by Your hands.

"9 But you are a chosen generation, a royal priesthood, a holy nation, His own special people, that you may proclaim the praises of Him who called you out of darkness into His marvelous light."
1 Peter 2:9

Lord, I declare the latter glory that will raise up the United States is greater than the former glory overshadowing this nation.

"[9] 'The glory of this latter temple shall be greater than the former,' says the LORD of hosts. 'And in this place I will give peace,' says the LORD of hosts."
Haggai 2:9

Chapter 13

PRAYERS FOR FOREIGNERS

Prayers for Foreigners

When God mentions foreigners, He commands that we treat them with love and respect. In Exodus 12, His Word says that, *"One law shall be for the native-born and for the stranger."* Likewise, Exodus 22 and 23 teaches not to deceive or oppress the foreigners or to cause them anxiety, *"For you know the heart of a stranger, because you were strangers in the land of Egypt."* Furthermore, Leviticus 19 establishes that, *"If a stranger dwells with you in your land, you shall not mistreat him."* Many of us come from other countries; hence, we understand the suffering that is experienced upon arrival in a foreign land. God is a Father of love and mercy. He makes no distinction between races, money, or social status. His deepest desire is for everyone to know His Son, Jesus Christ, and through Him, receive all the blessings He has for us. I know the Lord wants us to intercede on behalf of the foreigner; to pray and act in favor of their cause. Unite with me and let us believe for grace and favor, legal status, and the quick approval of requests and documentation for every foreigner, including you and your children.

In Your name, I declare legality over every foreigner living in this country. Lord, I ask You to forgive those who entered this country by illegally crossing the borders created by men. As You have forgiven us and given us citizenship in the heavenly Kingdom, I claim legal citizenship for those who have come to serve and honor this country. In the name of Jesus, I declare, decree, and establish that we are legal citizens of Heaven; therefore, if we are legal in Heaven, we are also legal on Earth.

"19Now, therefore, you are no longer strangers and foreigners, but fellow citizens with the saints and members of the household of God."
Ephesians 2:19

In the powerful name of Jesus, I activate the Angel of the Lord, with drawn sword, to destroy every opposition and stronghold that has paralyzed or delayed the process of obtaining legal residency, citizenship, and/or driver's licenses that rightfully belong to God's people.

"[13]And it came to pass, when Joshua was by Jericho, that he lifted his eyes and looked, and behold, a Man stood opposite him with His sword drawn in His hand..."
Joshua 5:13

Lord, I declare Your blessings upon me in the land where You have set my feet, and the people will know that Your name is exalted and glorified in the works of my hands.

"[8]The LORD will command the blessing on you in your storehouses and in all to which you set your hand, and He will bless you in the land which the LORD your God is giving you."
Deuteronomy 28:8

Lord, in Your name, I raise protective walls in favor of the foreigner. I declare laws of immigration that are just and which offer new opportunities for everyone living in the United States. I declare that immigrants are men and women of integrity, hard workers, and their only interest is to do what is right by this country. I declare that Jesus is their lawyer by excellence, and that He intercedes for them with power and authority.

"34 Who is he who condemns? It is Christ who died, and furthermore is also risen, who is even at the right hand of God, who also makes intercession for us."
Romans 8:34

Chapter 14

PRAYERS FOR ISRAEL

Prayers for Israel

The Word of God commands us to pray for Israel because this nation was chosen by God as the birthplace for His only begotten Son, Jesus, our Lord and Savior. For years, Israel has experienced wars, the holocaust, and countless dangers. Much blood has been spilled and countless martyrs have given their lives to protect the faith. They have suffered invasions and territorial struggles from enemies close and far, but in the midst of all this, God's protective hand has never left them. They have always been a blessed people. The Lord needs His Church to rise and pray for His chosen people. Your prayers can remove the veil that keeps the Israelites blinded to the light of the Gospel of the Kingdom. Your prayers can open their hearts and minds to receive the Savior they have been waiting for generations; the One who will manifest over their lives in a powerful way. Today I invite you to join me, and together, with God and the Church as one, let us pray for Israel until the glory of the Lord shines over that great nation.

Lord, I align my prayers to Your Word and declare the restoration of the House of Israel. If once Your people were scattered throughout the nations, You, Lord, will gather them back and settle them in their country. You have said that You will do it because of Your holy name and not because of their works. For this reason, today, I call out to the hills and mountains, to the springs and valleys, and declare that Israel rises once more, and it will be more fruitful and wealthy than ever. Lord, show Your power so Your people can know Jesus as their only Lord and Savior.

"[10]And I will multiply the number of people upon you, even the whole house of Israel. The towns will be inhabited and the ruins rebuilt. [11]I will increase the number of men and animals upon you, and they will be fruitful and become numerous. I will settle people on you as in the past and will make you prosper more than before. Then you will know that I am the LORD."

Ezekiel 36:10, 11 (NIV)

I proclaim peace over Israel and declare this to be a fortified city where Your name will be glorified. Lord, I loosen your peace over their government and authorities, in every street corner, and over each of Your chosen men and women.

"[3]Jerusalem is built like a city that is closely compacted together. [6]Pray for the peace of Jerusalem: 'May those who love you be secure.' [7]May there be peace within your walls and security within your citadels.' [8]For the sake of my brothers and friends, I will say, 'Peace be within you.' [9]For the sake of the house of the LORD our God, I will seek your prosperity."
Psalms 122:3, 6-9 (NIV)

Lord, thank You because Your Word says that Israel will proclaim the name of Jesus and worship You together with all the nations of the Earth.

"[21]To declare the name of the LORD in Zion, and His praise in Jerusalem, [22]When the peoples are gathered together, and the kingdoms, to serve the LORD."
Psalms 102:21, 22

....

....

....

....

Right now, I put into motion the prayer declared by our Lord, Jesus, over Israel, its people, and the Christian people. I declare that Jesus is one with us, as You are one with Him. I further declare that together, we walk in unison, and Your glory will be seen over Your people. I also pray for those who will know Jesus because of our testimony.

"[21]That they all may be one, as You, Father, are in Me, and I in You; that they also may be one in Us, that the world may believe that You sent Me. [22]And the glory which You gave Me I have given them, that they may be one just as We are one."
John 17:21, 22

Lord, I declare that You make the light of justice shine over Israel, and the rightful promises that belong to Your people will be fulfilled because You said it, and Your word is true.

"[6]He shall bring forth your righteousness as the light, and your justice as the noonday."
Psalms 37:6

Lord, in Your name, I call to action today's Nehemiahs. I call them forth to rise and restore the fallen wall of Jerusalem through prayer and intercession. I declare the God of Heaven and Earth will prosper them, and we, Your servants, will rise and build alongside because the enemies of Israel have no rights against us, Your people.

"[17]Then I said to them, 'You see the trouble we are in: Jerusalem lies in ruins, and its gates have been burned with fire. Come, let us rebuild the wall of Jerusalem, and we will no longer be in disgrace.' [20]I answered them by saying, 'The God of heaven will give us success. We his servants will start rebuilding...'"
Nehemiah 2:17, 20 (NIV)

Lord, I call forth every promise You made to Your people, Israel, and I declare their eyes will be opened to see Your glory, and their ears will attentive to hear Your promises.

"[5]Then the eyes of the blind shall be opened, and the ears of the deaf shall be unstopped."
Isaiah 35:5

Lord, I decree that no enemy army will make war against Your people. Every warfare strategy planned against Israel is annulled, destroyed, cancelled, and declared illegal. No weapon formed against Your people will prosper. In the name of Jesus, every weapon that rises against Israel becomes inoperative, right now!

"[4]He shall judge between the nations, and rebuke many people; they shall beat their swords into plowshares, and their spears into pruning hooks; nation shall not lift up sword against nation, neither shall they learn war anymore."
Isaiah 2:4

Lord, have mercy on Israel. Do not look on their stubbornness or sin. Remember Your faithful servants, and don't allow destruction to touch their generations or inheritance.

"[26]Therefore I prayed to the LORD, and said: 'O Lord GOD, do not destroy Your people and Your inheritance whom You have redeemed through Your greatness, whom You have brought out of Egypt with a mighty hand. [27]Remember Your servants, Abraham, Isaac, and Jacob; do not look on the stubbornness of this people, or on their wickedness or their sin."
Deuteronomy 9:26, 27

Lord, open the ears of Your chosen people and enable them to understand the truth and recognize the Lordship given by the Father to His Son, Jesus of Nazareth.

"[13]You shall fear the LORD your God and serve Him... [14]You shall not go after other gods, the gods of the peoples who are all around you."
Deuteronomy 6:13, 14

"[20]Which He worked in Christ when He raised Him from the dead and seated Him at His right hand in the heavenly places, [21]far above all principality and power and might and dominion, and every name that is named, not only in this age but also in that which is to come. [22]And He put all things under His feet, and gave Him to be head over all things to the church."
Ephesians 1:20-22